# Pocket Books

# Birds

## Kane Miller
A DIVISION OF EDC PUBLISHING

First American Edition 2015
Kane Miller, A Division of EDC Publishing

Copyright © Green Android Ltd 2014

For information contact:
Kane Miller, A Division of EDC Publishing
P.O. Box 470663
Tulsa, OK 74147-0663
www.kanemiller.com
www.edcpub.com
www.usbornebooksandmore.com

Please note that every effort has been made to check the accuracy of the information contained in this book, and to credit the copyright holders correctly. Green Android Ltd apologize for any unintentional errors or omissions, and would be happy to include revisions to content and/or acknowledgements in subsequent editions of this book.

Printed and bound in China, February 2015
1 2 3 4 5 6 7 8 9 10
Library of Congress Control Number: 2014950298
ISBN: 978-1-61067-385-3

Images © shutterstock.com: great tinamou © feathercollector;common ostrich © vblinov; greater rhea © poeticpenguin; southern cassowary © hin255; emu © pavels; north island brown kiwi © Eric Isselee; plain chachalaca © Warren Price Photography; helmeted guineafowl © Bogdan VASILESCU; California quail © Stubblefield Photography; wild turkey © Victoria Ditkovsky; western capercaillie © Mark Medcalf; sage grouse © Tom Reichner; gray partridge © Double Brow Imagery; red junglefowl © kowit sitthi; common pheasant © nawrocki; Indian peafowl © guentermanaus; magpie goose © Hugh Lansdown; Cape Barren goose © Tim Collins; graylag goose © EcoPrint; Canada goose © Elliotte Rusty Harold; Egyptian goose © Fabio Lotti; Muscovy duck © picturin; Mandarin duck © panda3800; mallard © LeonP; Eurasian teal © feathercollector; goosander © Tadas_Naujokaitis; black swan © Wallenrock; mute swan © Dan Kosmayer; red-throated loon © Wolfgang Kruck; great northern loon © Ian Maton; emperor penguin © Gentoo Multimedia Limited; adelie penguin © Sergey Tarasenko; chinstrap penguin © axily; macaroni penguin © Anton_Ivanov; little penguin © Khoroshunova Olga; humboldt penguin © Eric Gevaert; wandering albatross © Hugh Lansdown; southern giant petrel © AndreAnita; snow petrel © Rich Lindie; great crested grebe © Alexander Erdbeer; black-necked grebe © RazvanZinica; western grebe © Glenn Price; greater flamingo © zixian; lesser flamingo © Larry B. King; green heron © Paul Reeves Photography; gray heron © J Reineke; wood stork © smishonja; white stork © Matteo photos; scarlet ibis © Ilko Iliev; African spoonbill © Gerrit_de_Vries; great egret © Peter Gyure; shoebill © Sam DCruz; brown pelican © alexsvirid; blue-footed booby © Tadas_Jucys; great cormorant © Christian Musat; African darter © Chris Kruger; turkey vulture © claffra; western osprey © FloridaStock; harpy eagle © guentermanaus; golden eagle © Andy Dean Photography; northern goshawk © Pavel Mikoska; red kite © Scenic Shutterbug; bald eagle © Richard Lowthian; common buzzard © BogdanBoev; peregrine falcon © Mark Medcalf; common crane © Txanbelin; gray crowned crane © john michael evan potter; purple swamphen © TheRocky41; common moorhen © Arto Hakola; Eurasian oystercatcher © Stephen Rees; European herring gull © Wolfgang Kruck; little auk © BMJ; Atlantic puffin © Arnoud Quanjer; Burchell's sandgrouse © EcoPrint; rock dove © Marco Barone; common wood pigeon © Menno Schaefer; Eurasian collared dove © gregg williams; common cuckoo © SW_Stock; greater roadrunner © Steve Byland; red-crested turaco © Tramont_ana; gray parrot © Mikael Damkier; red-and-green macaw © apiguide; rainbow lorikeet © jurra8; sulphur-crested cockatoo © Nicky Rhodes; galah © Jordan Tan; western barn owl © Mark Bridger; snowy owl © Daniel Hebert; great horned owl © Stephen Mcsweeny; tawny owl © S.Cooper Digital; European nightjar © Dmytro Pylypenko; tawny frogmouth © Mark Eastment; ruby-throated hummingbird © Sari ONeal; sword-billed hummingbird © JNB Photography; common swift © Florian Andronache; speckled mousebird © Jan Hattingh; great hornbill © apiguide; violaceous trogon © BMJ; resplendent quetzal © worldswildlifewonders; common kingfisher © assoonas; pied kingfisher © Gerrit_de_Vries; laughing kookaburra © feathercollector ; great spotted woodpecker © Menno Schaefer; acorn woodpecker © WLB79; emerald toucanet © evantravels; keel-billed toucan © Eduardo Rivero; eastern kingbird © Feng Yu; superb fairywren © CoolR; New Zealand fantail © Rob Harland; blue jay © Steve Byland; northern raven © Dirk Ott; Japanese waxwing © Hawk777; great tit © Kirk Norbury; Eurasian wren © Paul Reeves Photography; European robin © CliffP; house sparrow © Rob Christiaans; Java sparrow © Stubblefield Photography; northern cardinal © Elliotte Rusty Harold; painted bunting © Steve Byland.

# Introducing birds

There are around 10,000 different types of birds worldwide. They range from tiny hummingbirds to huge ostriches. About a fifth of all birds undertake seasonal migrations. Each year they travel from one part of the world to another and then back again. As the seasons change they will migrate to areas with more food resources. All birds lay eggs and most birds are able to fly.

**Canada geese travel up to 1500 miles per day during their annual migration.**

**The red-and-green macaw has brightly colored feathers.**

**The bill of a northern raven is shaped for tearing at meat.**

## Characteristics of birds

Birds have three characteristics that make them different from other animal groups.

Birds are vertebrates, which means they have a backbone. Unlike most other vertebrates, birds have a light skeleton filled with hollows. This keeps them lightweight for flight.

All birds have feathers. Feathers are used for warmth and protection, for decoration and to help birds control their flight.

All birds have a bill. This bony projection forms their mouths. Bills are shaped for the bird's diet.

# How to use this book

**The pages of this book include concise information and key features on birds from around the world.**

**Common name** (this is the name mostly used)

**Scientific name** (this is the name of the animal used by scientists)

**Factfile** (see opposite page)

### Southern Cassowary
*Casuarius casuarius*

Birds
Flightless birds
Rheas, cassowaries and emus

**Bird groups** (see pages 6-7)

**Color photograph**

#### Factfile

| | |
|---|---|
| **Habitat** | Rain forest |
| **Distribution** | Indonesia, New Guinea, Australia |
| **Height** | 4 to 5.5 ft |
| **Weight** | 65 to 125 lb |
| **Life span** | Up to 30 years |
| **Migration** | Nonmigrant |

**Diet** Southern cassowaries mostly eat fallen fruit and fruit on low branches, but will also feed on fungi, insects, frogs, snakes and other small animals.

**Fact** To protect themselves, southern cassowaries will kick at anything that comes too close. Their three-toed feet have a 5-inch sharp middle claw.

**Conservation status** Vulnerable

**Conservation status** (see opposite page)

**Page number** 10

Macaroni penguins

4

# Factfile

Each page comes with a detailed factfile containing descriptions, information, facts and figures.

**Habitat**
This indicates the environment that the bird lives in. Some birds will live in many different habitats.

**Distribution**
This describes where in the world the bird is found in its natural habitat.

**Length/Height**
A measurement of the bird's body.

**Diet**
A description of the food that the bird eats and where it gets the food.

**Weight**
A measurement of the weight of the bird.

**Life span**
This is the average natural length of the bird's life.

**Migration**
An indication of the type of migration for each bird. Migratory birds travel long distances around the world. Partial migrant birds do not all migrate, sometimes only the females migrate. Nonmigrant birds do not travel between habitats. They are sometimes called sedentary birds.

**Fact**
Every factfile comes with an interesting fact about each bird.

# Conservation status

Each animal in this book has been given a conservation status. This status indicates the threat of extinction to the species in its native home.

**Not evaluated**
The animals within this category have not yet been evaluated for their conservation status.

**Least concern**
This is the lowest risk category. Animals in this category are widespread and abundant.

**Near threatened**
The animals in this category are likely to become endangered in the near future.

**Vulnerable**
There is a high risk that animals within this category will become endangered in the wild.

**Endangered**
There is a high risk that animals within this category will become extinct in the wild.

**Critically endangered**
There is an extremely high risk of animals in this category becoming extinct in the wild.

# Bird groups

There are many ways to classify and group birds. In this book we have divided the birds into five separate groups (although there will be some that cross over into more than one group).

## Birds of prey
### Over 300 species

The large birds in this group are all accomplished hunters. They have acute eyesight, strong legs, and sharp talons and bills. They are found almost worldwide, but are most common in open countryside in warm areas.

## Flightless birds
### Around 40 species

Although birds in this group are unable to fly, many can run at high speeds. Some flightless birds, such as penguins, are excellent swimmers and divers. Their wings have evolved into narrow paddles that they use to push themselves through water.

## Nightjars and relatives
### Around 125 species

Nightjars are long-winged nocturnal birds. They can be seen looking for food at dusk and dawn. They have feathers in mottled brown and grey. Many species are known for their loud distinctive calls.

## Gamebirds and waterbirds
### Over 800 species

Game birds are a group of ground-dwelling birds including chickens, guinea fowl, pheasants, peafowl and turkeys. Waterbirds have evolved particular adaptations which make them well suited to wet habitats.

**Male Indian peafowl display their magnificent tail feathers.**

A bald eagle's vision is five times sharper than our own.

## Perching birds and relatives
### Over 8,000 species

Perching birds are known for their complex vocalizations and songs, and their unique foot structure. Their feet have four long, thin toes. Three toes face forward and one faces backward. Perching birds have a variety of close relatives that share some of their characteristics. These relatives include tropical birds such as parrots and toucans.

A blue jay's song can last for more than 2 minutes.

# Contents

**Flightless birds**

| | |
|---|---|
| Ostriches | 8 |
| Rheas, cassowaries and emus | 9 |
| Kiwis | 12 |
| Penguins | 13 |

**Game birds and waterbirds**

| | |
|---|---|
| Game birds | 19 |
| Waterbirds | 31 |

**Birds of prey**

| | |
|---|---|
| Diurnal birds of prey | 73 |
| Nocturnal birds of prey | 82 |

**Nightjars and relatives**

| | |
|---|---|
| Nightjars | 86 |
| Frogmouths | 87 |

**Perching birds and relatives**

| | |
|---|---|
| Perching birds | 88 |
| Parrots | 101 |
| Cuckoos and turacos | 106 |
| Hummingbirds and swifts | 109 |
| Hornbills and trogons | 112 |
| Woodpeckers and kingfishers | 115 |
| Toucans | 120 |
| Mousebirds | 122 |
| Pigeons and doves | 123 |
| **Glossary** | **126** |
| **Index** | **128** |

# Common Ostrich

*Struthio camelus*

Birds

Flightless birds

Ostriches

## Factfile

| | |
|---|---|
| **Habitat** | Savannah, woodland, desert, grassland |
| **Distribution** | Africa |
| **Height** | 7 to 9 ft |
| **Weight** | 220 to 350 lb |
| **Life span** | 30 to 40 years |
| **Migration** | Nonmigrant |

**Diet** Ostriches mostly eat plants, especially roots, leaves and seeds, but will also eat insects, snakes, lizards or rodents that come within reach.

**Fact** An ostrich group, called a herd, is generally made up of about 12 birds. Male ostriches compete with one another for control of the group.

**Conservation status**    Least concern

8

# Greater Rhea

## *Rhea americana*

## Factfile

| | |
|---|---|
| **Habitat** | Grassland, woodland, pampas |
| **Distribution** | South America |
| **Length** | 3 to 5 ft |
| **Weight** | 50 to 55 lb |
| **Life span** | Up to 15 years |
| **Migration** | Nonmigrant |

**Diet**
Greater rheas are opportunistic eaters. They feed mainly on plant matter including plants, fruit and seeds, but also eat insects, lizards and small game.

**Fact**
Although the large wings of the greater rheas are useless for flight, they are used for balance and for changing direction as the bird runs.

| **Conservation status** | **Near threatened** |
|---|---|

# Southern Cassowary

*Casuarius casuarius*

Birds

Flightless birds

Rheas, cassowaries and emus

## Factfile

| | |
|---|---|
| **Habitat** | Rain forest |
| **Distribution** | Indonesia, New Guinea, Australia |
| **Height** | 4 to 5.5 ft |
| **Weight** | 65 to 125 lb |
| **Life span** | Up to 30 years |
| **Migration** | Nonmigrant |

**Diet** Southern cassowaries mostly eat fallen fruit and fruit on low branches, but will also feed on fungi, insects, frogs, snakes and other small animals.

**Fact** To protect themselves, southern cassowaries will kick at anything that comes too close. Their three-toed feet have a 5-inch sharp middle claw.

**Conservation status**   **Vulnerable**

# Emu
*Dromaius novaehollandiae*

## Factfile

| | |
|---|---|
| **Habitat** | Savannah, forest, grassland |
| **Distribution** | Australia |
| **Height** | 4.9 to 6.2 ft |
| **Weight** | 66 to 120 lb |
| **Life span** | Up to 19 years |
| **Migration** | Nonmigrant |

**Diet** Emus eat a wide variety of plants. They also eat insects such as grasshoppers and crickets, ladybugs, caterpillars, moth larvae and ants.

**Fact** Emus have tiny, relatively useless wings, but their legs are long and extremely strong. They can sprint at speeds of around 30 miles per hour.

**Conservation status**  **Least concern**

# North Island Brown Kiwi

*Apteryx mantelli*

## Factfile

| | |
|---|---|
| **Habitat** | Subtropical and temperate forest |
| **Distribution** | North Island of New Zealand |
| **Length** | Up to 12 in |
| **Weight** | 4.8 to 6.2 lb |
| **Life span** | Up to 30 years |
| **Migration** | Nonmigrant |

**Diet** Kiwis eat worms, spiders, insects, berries and seeds. Their excellent sense of smell can detect food among leaves, logs and soft soil.

**Fact** Female kiwis lay very large eggs, which can be up to a quarter of their own body weight, but it is the male who looks after the eggs and chicks.

**Conservation status**      **Endangered**

# Emperor Penguin
### *Aptenodytes forsteri*

## Factfile

| | |
|---|---|
| **Habitat** | Open ice, frozen land |
| **Distribution** | Antarctica |
| **Height** | 3.6 to 4.1 ft |
| **Weight** | 48 to 82 lb |
| **Life span** | Up to 20 years |
| **Migration** | Nonmigrant |

**Diet** Emperor penguins eat fish and squid. They have a spiny tongue and powerful jaws that help to grip their prey before swallowing it whole.

**Fact** After the female emperor penguin lays an egg the male balances it on his feet and keeps it warm in a brood pouch until it hatches.

**Conservation status**     **Least concern**

13

# Adélie Penguin

*Pygoscelis adeliae*

Birds

Flightless birds

Penguins

## Factfile

| | |
|---|---|
| **Habitat** | Rocky coast, ice floes, islands |
| **Distribution** | Antarctica |
| **Length** | 18 to 24 in |
| **Weight** | 10 to 11 lb |
| **Life span** | Up to 20 years |
| **Migration** | Migrant |

**Diet** Adélie penguins feed mostly on Antarctic krill, ice krill or sea krill, but they will also supplement their diet with small fish and squid.

**Fact** Adélie penguins are known for forming enormous breeding colonies. Some of the colonies can contain more than half a million penguins.

**Conservation status**      Least concern

# Chinstrap Penguin
### *Pygoscelis antarcticus*

## Factfile

| | |
|---|---|
| **Habitat** | Rocky slopes, headlands, high cliff edges |
| **Distribution** | Antarctica |
| **Length** | 27 to 30 in |
| **Weight** | 6.5 to 10 lb |
| **Life span** | 15 to 20 years |
| **Migration** | Migrant |

**Diet** Chinstrap penguins will swim up to 18 miles searching for food. Their diet consists almost exclusively of krill with a small amount of squid and fish.

**Fact** Although small, they have the courage to fight off larger penguin species and are known as the most aggressive of all penguin species.

| **Conservation status** | **Least concern** |
|---|---|

# Macaroni Penguin

*Eudyptes chrysolophus*

## Factfile

| | |
|---|---|
| **Habitat** | Rocky slopes |
| **Distribution** | Chile, South Atlantic, south Indian Ocean |
| **Length** | 25 to 30 in |
| **Weight** | 11 to 13 lb |
| **Life span** | 15 to 20 years |
| **Migration** | Migrant |

**Diet** Macaroni penguins feed mainly on krill, but will occasionally eat other small crustaceans, fish and squid. They hunt at depths of up to 195 feet.

**Fact** Although the female macaroni penguin lays 2 eggs, the second egg is always the largest and is often the only one to hatch successfully.

| **Conservation status** | **Vulnerable** |
|---|---|

# Little Penguin

*Eudyptula minor*

## Factfile

| | |
|---|---|
| **Habitat** | Sandy or rocky coastline |
| **Distribution** | Southern Australia, New Zealand |
| **Length** | 11.8 to 15.8 in |
| **Weight** | 2.4 to 2.6 lb |
| **Life span** | Up to 7 years |
| **Migration** | Partial migrant |

**Diet** Little penguins feed on small fish, squid and krill. They hunt near the surface of the water for fish such as pilchards, anchovies and garfish.

**Fact** Little penguins face a number of threats. On the mainland, dogs, cats and foxes pose the greatest threat by attacking both adults and chicks.

**Conservation status**      **Least concern**

# Humboldt Penguin

*Spheniscus humboldti*

Birds

Flightless birds

Penguins

## Factfile

| | |
|---|---|
| **Habitat** | Desert, rocky shores |
| **Distribution** | Western South America |
| **Length** | 22 to 26 in |
| **Weight** | 10 to 11 lb |
| **Life span** | 15 to 20 years |
| **Migration** | Nonmigrant |

**Diet** Humboldt penguins hunt in groups in shallow water, circling their prey before attacking. They feed on fish such as anchovies and sardines.

**Fact** Humboldt penguins have two layers of feathers: a down layer for insulation and a waterproof layer that prevents cold water reaching their skin.

| **Conservation status** | **Vulnerable** |
|---|---|

# Gray Partridge
*Perdix perdix*

## Factfile

| | |
|---|---|
| **Habitat** | Farmland, steppe, wood edge |
| **Distribution** | Europe, Asia, North America |
| **Length** | 11.2 to 13 in |
| **Weight** | 13.5 to 17.6 oz |
| **Life span** | Up to 3 years |
| **Migration** | Nonmigrant |

**Diet** Most of the gray partridge's diet is made up of seeds and grains, but the young will also eat insects as an essential protein supply.

**Fact** Gray partridge hens produce some of the largest clutches of any bird species. Their average clutch size is 16-18 eggs, but can be up to 22 eggs.

**Conservation status**      **Least concern**

# Great Tinamou

*Tinamus major*

## Factfile

| | |
|---|---|
| **Habitat** | Subtropical and tropical forest |
| **Distribution** | Central and South America |
| **Length** | 16 to 19 in |
| **Weight** | Up to 2.4 lb |
| **Life span** | Up to 10 years |
| **Migration** | Nonmigrant |

**Diet** The great tinamou finds all of its food on the forest floor. It feeds mostly on berries, fruit and seeds, but insects and invertebrates are also eaten.

**Fact** After the female great tinamou lays her eggs she will leave the male to look after them. The male rears the chicks for around 20 days.

**Conservation status**     **Least concern**

20

# Common Pheasant

*Phasianus colchicus*

## Factfile

| | |
|---|---|
| **Habitat** | Farmland, prairie |
| **Distribution** | North America, Europe, Asia |
| **Length** | 19.7 to 27.6 in |
| **Weight** | 1.1 to 6 lb |
| **Life span** | 1 to 2 years |
| **Migration** | Nonmigrant |

**Diet** Pheasants are omnivorous ground feeders. Their varied diet includes grains, seeds, shoots and berries, as well as insects and small invertebrates.

**Fact** Pheasants prefer to run when they sense trouble. However, when startled, they can fly upward, reaching speeds of nearly 40 miles per hour.

| **Conservation status** | **Least concern** |
|---|---|

# California Quail

*Callipepla californica*

Birds

Game birds and waterbirds

Game birds

## Factfile

| | |
|---|---|
| **Habitat** | Brushy chaparral, canyons, open woodland |
| **Distribution** | North America, Hawaii, Chile, Australasia |
| **Length** | 9.4 to 10.6 in |
| **Weight** | 4.9 to 8.1 oz |
| **Life span** | Up to 7 years |
| **Migration** | Nonmigrant |

**Diet** The diet of the California quail is variable. They eat seeds and plant parts such as buds. They will sometimes eat a few insects too.

**Fact** The California quail's head plume, or topknot, looks like a single large feather, but it is actually a cluster of six overlapping feathers.

**Conservation status**     Least concern

# Greater Sage-grouse

### *Centrocercus urophasianus*

## Factfile

| | |
|---|---|
| **Habitat** | Foothills, plains, mountain slopes |
| **Distribution** | North America |
| **Length** | 22 to 29.5 in |
| **Weight** | 4 to 6.4 lb |
| **Life span** | Up to 7 years |
| **Migration** | Nonmigrant |

**Diet** The majority of the greater sage-grouse's diet comes from sagebrush. The birds will also forage on the ground for insects and other plants.

**Fact** To attract a mate the males will gather at display grounds (which are called leeks) and strut around, displaying their beautiful plumage.

| **Conservation status** | **Endangered** |
|---|---|

# Burchell's Sandgrouse

*Pterocles burchelli*

## Factfile

| | |
|---|---|
| **Habitat** | Grassland, scrubland |
| **Distribution** | Africa |
| **Length** | 9 to 10.5 in |
| **Weight** | 5.6 to 7 oz |
| **Life span** | Unknown |
| **Migration** | Nonmigrant |

**Diet** The Burchell's sandgrouse mainly eats seeds, especially of legumes, doing most of its foraging in pairs or small flocks during the day.

**Fact** The belly feathers of the sandgrouse can hold water. They transport it to their chicks as the nests are often far from water sources.

**Conservation status**   **Least concern**

# Helmeted Guineafowl
*Numida meleagris*

## Factfile

| | |
|---|---|
| **Habitat** | Savannah, farmland |
| **Distribution** | Africa (south of Sahara) |
| **Length** | 21 to 23 in |
| **Weight** | 2.2 to 3.3 lb |
| **Life span** | Up to 12 years |
| **Migration** | Nonmigrant |

**Diet** Helmeted guineafowl eat a varied diet, including seeds, fruit, spiders, worms, insects, frogs, lizards, snakes and even some small mammals.

**Fact** Helmeted guineafowl are monomorphic and monochromatic. This means that both the male and female look alike and behave in similar ways.

| Conservation status | Least concern |
|---|---|

25

# Wild Turkey
## *Meleagris gallopavo*

## Factfile

| | |
|---|---|
| **Habitat** | Open woodland |
| **Distribution** | North America |
| **Length** | 3.25 to 3.75 ft |
| **Weight** | 5.5 to 24 lb |
| **Life span** | Up to 4 years |
| **Migration** | Nonmigrant |

**Diet** Wild turkeys eat plant matter which they forage for in flocks, mostly on the ground, but sometimes climbing into shrubs or low trees for fruit.

**Fact** Wild turkeys sleep perched high up in tree branches, safe from predators such as coyotes, foxes, skunks, raccoons, snakes and dogs.

**Conservation status**     **Least concern**

# Western Capercaillie
*Tetrao urogallus*

## Factfile

| | |
|---|---|
| **Habitat** | Forest |
| **Distribution** | Europe, Asia |
| **Length** | 21 to 33 in |
| **Weight** | 8.4 to 14 lb |
| **Life span** | Up to 4 years |
| **Migration** | Nonmigrant |

**Diet** During the summer these birds feed on bilberry leaves, berries, shoots and seeds. In the winter they mostly eat conifer needles and buds.

**Fact** The male western capercaillies do not like people, dogs or cars, and they will often rush at them in attack mode if they feel threatened.

**Conservation status**      Least concern

# Red Junglefowl
*Gallus gallus*

**Birds**

**Game birds and waterbirds**

**Game birds**

## Factfile

| | |
|---|---|
| **Habitat** | Thick secondary forest |
| **Distribution** | South and Southeast Asia |
| **Length** | 27 to 31 in |
| **Weight** | 1.1 to 3.3 lb |
| **Life span** | Up to 10 years |
| **Migration** | Nonmigrant |

**Diet** The diet of the red junglefowl is mostly made up of insects, especially termites and winged ants, corn, soybeans, worms, grasses and various grains.

**Fact** Red junglefowl can be distinguished from other types of chickens by the two white patches, shaped like ears, on either side of the head.

| **Conservation status** | **Least concern** |
|---|---|

28

# Plain Chachalaca

*Ortalis vetula*

## Factfile

| | |
|---|---|
| **Habitat** | Forest |
| **Distribution** | North and Central America |
| **Length** | 19 to 24 in |
| **Weight** | 10.5 to 24 oz |
| **Life span** | Up to 9 years |
| **Migration** | Nonmigrant |

**Diet** The plain chachalaca feeds on fruit and berries, seeds, leaves, buds and flowers. They will sometimes eat insects, spiders and some small snails.

**Fact** The plain chachalaca spends most of its time foraging in trees. It is often seen feeding in precarious positions, including upside down!

**Conservation status**          **Least concern**

# Indian Peafowl
*Pavo cristatus*

## Factfile

| | |
|---|---|
| **Habitat** | Forest, orchards, cultivated areas |
| **Distribution** | South Asia |
| **Length** | 35 to 50 in |
| **Weight** | 8.75 to 13 lb |
| **Life span** | Up to 20 years |
| **Migration** | Nonmigrant |

**Diet** Peafowls forage for food early in the morning and late at night. They eat grains, insects, reptiles, mammals, berries and some cultivated crops.

**Fact** Each male has around 100 to 150 tail feathers. They are approximately 5 feet long. The circular pattern on these feathers is called an eyespot.

**Conservation status**      Least concern

# Magpie Goose

*Anseranas semipalmata*

## Factfile

| | |
|---|---|
| **Habitat** | Floodplain, wet grassland |
| **Distribution** | New Guinea, north Australia |
| **Length** | 27.5 to 35.5 in |
| **Weight** | Up to 6.6 lb |
| **Life span** | Up to 30 years |
| **Migration** | Partial migrant |

**Diet** Magpie geese eat many different plants and seeds. They will graze and dig, pushing down any tall grasses with their feet in order to reach seeds.

**Fact** When traveling they often move in large flocks of several thousand. Pair bonds are usually kept for life but males may mate two females.

**Conservation status**      **Least concern**

# Cape Barren Goose

*Cereopsis novaehollandiae*

## Factfile

| | |
|---|---|
| **Habitat** | Grassy islands off the Australian coast |
| **Distribution** | South Australia |
| **Length** | 30 to 40 in |
| **Weight** | 7 to 15 lb |
| **Life span** | Up to 15 years |
| **Migration** | Nonmigrant |

**Diet** The cape barren goose has a diet made up mostly of the common island tussock grass, spear grass, and various herbs and succulents.

**Fact** On the ground these birds are fairly quiet unless alarmed, but in flight the male makes a high-pitched, harsh trumpeted "ark, ark-ark" sound.

| **Conservation status** | **Least concern** |
|---|---|

# Greylag Goose

*Anser anser*

## Factfile

| | |
|---|---|
| **Habitat** | Lakes, coast, marsh |
| **Distribution** | Europe, Greenland, Asia, North America |
| **Length** | 30 to 35 in |
| **Weight** | 5 to 10 lb |
| **Life span** | Up to 21 years |
| **Migration** | Migrant |

**Diet** Greylag geese are mainly vegetarian. Their diet includes grasses, leaves, roots, stems, and the fruit and sprouts of numerous plant species.

**Fact** They often fly in a "V" formation. This helps them to save energy because each bird shares the air current created by the bird in front of it.

**Conservation status**      **Least concern**

# Canada Goose

*Branta canadensis*

## Factfile

| | |
|---|---|
| **Habitat** | Lakes, ponds, rivers, grassland, marsh |
| **Distribution** | North America, Europe, Asia, New Zealand |
| **Length** | 30 to 40 in |
| **Weight** | 6 to 18 lb |
| **Life span** | Up to 24 years |
| **Migration** | Migrant |

**Diet** Canada geese are herbivorous grazers. Their natural diet consists of tender grasses, seeds, grains, sedges and other aquatic vegetation.

**Fact** If the wind conditions are suitable when they migrate, a flock of Canada geese can travel a distance of over 1500 miles in just 24 hours.

| **Conservation status** | **Least concern** |
|---|---|

# Egyptian Goose

*Alopochen aegyptiacus*

## Factfile

| | |
|---|---|
| **Habitat** | Most wetland habitats |
| **Distribution** | Africa (south of Sahara) |
| **Length** | 25 to 29 in |
| **Weight** | 3.3 to 5.3 lb |
| **Life span** | Up to 14 years |
| **Migration** | Nonmigrant |

**Diet** Egyptian geese feed on plant matter, including grasses, seeds, shoots, grains and crops. Sometimes they also eat worms, locusts or winged termites.

**Fact** These geese live in large flocks as a defense against predators since more individuals may warn when a potential predator is spotted.

| Conservation status | Least concern |
|---|---|

# Muscovy Duck

*Carina moschata*

Birds

Game birds and waterbirds

Waterbirds

## Factfile

| | |
|---|---|
| **Habitat** | Rivers, ponds, wooded swamp, wetland |
| **Distribution** | Central America to central South America |
| **Length** | 26 to 33 in |
| **Weight** | 5 to 15 lb |
| **Life span** | 7 to 8 years |
| **Migration** | Nonmigrant |

**Diet** Muscovy ducks eat plant material obtained by grazing or dabbling in shallow water, and insects, fish, reptiles and some small mammals.

**Fact** Muscovy ducks do not swim as often as most other ducks because their oil glands are not as well developed, which means their feathers can fray easily.

| **Conservation status** | **Least concern** |
|---|---|

# Mandarin Duck
*Aix galericulata*

## Factfile

| | |
|---|---|
| **Habitat** | Wooded ponds, swamp, streams |
| **Distribution** | China, Russia, Siberia, Japan |
| **Length** | 15.7 to 19.5 in |
| **Weight** | 15 to 24 oz |
| **Life span** | 6 to 7 years |
| **Migration** | Partial migrant |

**Diet** Mandarin ducks mostly feed on grains. They also consume a lot of aquatic vegetation. They occasionally eat fish, land snails and bugs.

**Fact** They build nests in tree holes. Once the eggs hatch, the mother calls the ducklings from the ground and they leap from the nest to the ground.

**Conservation status** — **Least concern**

37

# Mallard
*Anas platyrhynchos*

## Factfile

| | |
|---|---|
| **Habitat** | Most wetland habitats |
| **Distribution** | North America, Europe, Greenland, Asia |
| **Length** | 19.7 to 25.6 in |
| **Weight** | 2.2 to 3.3 lb |
| **Life span** | 3 to 5 years |
| **Migration** | Partial migrant |

**Diet** Mallards are foragers. They eat seeds and aquatic vegetation. During the breeding season they also eat insect larvae, earthworms, snails and shrimp.

**Fact** Mallards are often found in city and suburban park ponds. They can become very tame and approachable because of constant feeding by visitors.

| **Conservation status** | **Least concern** |
|---|---|

# Eurasian Teal

*Anas crecca*

## Factfile

| | |
|---|---|
| **Habitat** | Wetland, reed beds, lakes, ponds |
| **Distribution** | North America, Europe, Asia, Africa |
| **Length** | 12.5 to 15.5 in |
| **Weight** | 11 to 14 oz |
| **Life span** | Up to 3 years |
| **Migration** | Partial migrant |

**Diet** The Eurasian teal has a varied diet that includes insects, larvae, worms, mollusks and crustaceans, and vegetation including various seeds.

**Fact** Eurasian teal are rapid flyers, flapping their wings incredibly quickly. This often gives the impression that they are constantly in a rush!

**Conservation status**        **Least concern**

# Common Merganser

*Merges merganser*

## Factfile

| | |
|---|---|
| **Habitat** | Lakes, rivers, lagoons, marsh |
| **Distribution** | North America, Europe, Asia |
| **Length** | 22 to 27 in |
| **Weight** | 2.5 to 3.6 lb |
| **Life span** | Up to 10 years |
| **Migration** | Partial migrant |

**Diet** Common mergansers feed largely on small and medium-sized fish, such as salmon and trout. Occasionally they will hunt and catch larger fish such as pike.

**Fact** Common mergansers have bodies that are adapted for rapid underwater swimming and flight. They can reach speeds of 55 miles per hour in the air.

| Conservation status | Least concern |
|---|---|

# Black Swan
## *Cygnus atratus*

## Factfile

| | |
|---|---|
| **Habitat** | Lakes, rivers, wetland, coast |
| **Distribution** | Australia, New Zealand |
| **Length** | 3.6 to 4.6 ft |
| **Weight** | 8.1 to 19.1 lb |
| **Life span** | Up to 40 years |
| **Migration** | Nomadic |

**Diet** Black swans are almost exclusively herbivorous, meaning they only eat plants. They have a diet consisting of aquatic and marshland plants.

**Fact** When a group of swans is on the ground they are called a bank, however, when they are in flight they are referred to as a wedge.

**Conservation status** — Least concern

41

# Mute Swan

*Cygnus olor*

Birds

Game birds and waterbirds

Waterbirds

## Factfile

| | |
|---|---|
| **Habitat** | Most river habitats, some lakes and ponds |
| **Distribution** | North America, Europe, Africa, Asia, Australia |
| **Length** | 4.5 to 5.3 ft |
| **Weight** | 17 to 32 lb |
| **Life span** | 5 to 6 years |
| **Migration** | Partial migrant |

**Diet**   Mute swans are omnivores, eating both plants and animals. They eat water plants and algae with the occasional insect, fish and crustacean.

**Fact**   One can guess from the name that mute swans are not very vocal. They do, however, make a loud hissing sound when they feel threatened.

| Conservation status | Least concern |
|---|---|

42

# Red-throated Loon
*Gavia stellata*

## Factfile

| | |
|---|---|
| **Habitat** | Shallow ponds and lakes |
| **Distribution** | North America, Europe, Greenland, Asia |
| **Length** | 22 to 27.5 in |
| **Weight** | 2.2 to 5.5 lb |
| **Life span** | Up to 20 years |
| **Migration** | Migrant |

**Diet** These birds are primarily fish eaters, but may feed on mollusks, crustaceans, aquatic invertebrates, amphibians, insects or plant material.

**Fact** The red-throated loon can dive to depths of 30 feet and snatch its prey in its long bill. They can stay underwater for a minute and a half.

**Conservation status**      **Least concern**

43

# Common Loon
*Gavia immer*

## Factfile

| | |
|---|---|
| **Habitat** | Coast, large lakes |
| **Distribution** | North America, Greenland, western Europe |
| **Length** | 2 to 3 ft |
| **Weight** | 6.5 to 12 lb |
| **Life span** | Up to 9 years |
| **Migration** | Migrant |

**Diet** Common loons feed on pike, perch, sunfish, trout and bass in fresh water, and rockfish, sea trout, herring and flounder in saltwater.

**Fact** Common loons are very well known birds in Canada. They are even featured on one side of the "loonie," the Canadian one-dollar coin.

**Conservation status**     **Least concern**

# Brown Pelican

*Pelecanus occidentalis*

## Factfile

| | |
|---|---|
| **Habitat** | Coast, lagoons |
| **Distribution** | The Americas, Caribbean |
| **Length** | 3.3 to 5 ft |
| **Weight** | Over 7.7 lb |
| **Life span** | 15 to 25 years |
| **Migration** | Partial migrant |

**Diet** Brown pelicans eat medium-sized fish. They catch the fish by diving and using a pouch in their throat like a fishing net.

**Fact** Brown pelicans enjoy living alongside humans. They are often seen at fishing ports feeding on fish scraps discarded by fishermen.

**Conservation status**     **Least concern**

# Blue-footed Booby

*Sula nebouxii*

## Factfile

| | |
|---|---|
| **Habitat** | Coast |
| **Distribution** | Central and South America, Galápagos Islands |
| **Length** | 32 to 34 in |
| **Weight** | 2.5 to 4.5 lb |
| **Life span** | Up to 17 years |
| **Migration** | Partial migrant |

**Diet** The blue-footed booby mainly feeds on fish such as flying fish, sardines, anchovies and mackerel. They also occasionally eat squid.

**Fact** During mating rituals the male blue-footed booby takes great pride in showing off his feet to females. The bluer the feet, the more attractive the male.

**Conservation status**     Least concern

# Great Cormorant

*Phalacrocorax carbo*

## Factfile

| | |
|---|---|
| **Habitat** | Coast, lakes |
| **Distribution** | North America, Europe, Asia, Africa, Australia |
| **Length** | 33 to 36 in |
| **Weight** | 5.7 to 8.2 lb |
| **Life span** | Up to 11 years |
| **Migration** | Partial migrant |

**Diet** Great cormorants eat fish, such as sculpins, capelin and gadids, as well as some crustaceans, amphibians, mollusks and occasional nestlings.

**Fact** To catch fish they dive from the surface of the water and chase their prey underwater. They grab the fish in their bills, without spearing them.

**Conservation status**     **Least concern**

# African Darter

*Anhinga rufa*

## Factfile

| | |
|---|---|
| **Habitat** | Swamp, lakes |
| **Distribution** | Africa, Asia, Australia, New Guinea |
| **Length** | 33 to 38 in |
| **Weight** | 2.2 to 4.4 lb |
| **Life span** | Up to 15 years |
| **Migration** | Partial migrant |

**Diet** The African darter's diet is primarily made up of fish, but they will also supplement this with some aquatic animals, such as snakes, frogs and crustaceans.

**Fact** Darters are effective aquatic hunters. They use their sharp bills to spear fish underwater before flipping them in the air and swallowing them headfirst.

**Conservation status**    **Near threatened**

48

# Purple Swamphen
### *Porphyrio porphyrio*

## Factfile

| | |
|---|---|
| **Habitat** | Lakes, marsh, rivers, swamp, wetland |
| **Distribution** | Europe, Asia, Australia, Africa |
| **Length** | 15 to 20 in |
| **Weight** | 1.1 to 2.8 lb |
| **Life span** | Up to 22 years |
| **Migration** | Nonmigrant |

**Diet** The diet of the purple swamphen includes the soft shoots of reeds or rushes, leaves, roots, and small animals such as frogs, snails and insects.

**Fact** Purple swamphens are very aggressive animals and will bully many other birds. They are known to steal eggs and will even eat ducklings.

**Conservation status**      **Least concern**

# Common Moorhen

*Gallinula chloropus*

Birds

Game birds and waterbirds

Waterbirds

## Factfile

| | |
|---|---|
| **Habitat** | Lakes, marsh, rivers, swamp, wetland |
| **Distribution** | Worldwide (except Antarctica) |
| **Length** | 12 to 15 in |
| **Weight** | 6.8 to 18 oz |
| **Life span** | Up to 3 years |
| **Migration** | Partial migrant |

**Diet** Common moorhens feed while walking on floating plants. They eat seeds, plant material, algae, small fish, tadpoles, insects, snails and worms.

**Fact** Moorhens are social birds that gather in flocks of 15–30 individuals. An older adult male is generally the dominant member of the flock.

**Conservation status**      **Least concern**

# Eurasian Oystercatcher
*Haematopus ostralegus*

## Factfile

| | |
|---|---|
| **Habitat** | Coast, estuaries |
| **Distribution** | Europe, Africa, Asia |
| **Length** | 16 to 19 in |
| **Weight** | 14 to 28 oz |
| **Life span** | Up to 12 years |
| **Migration** | Migrant |

**Diet** The Eurasian oystercatcher feeds mainly on mussels and other mollusks such as limpets and whelks, crabs, earthworms and insect larvae.

**Fact** These oystercatchers open mussel shells that are slightly ajar by prodding their slender bills into the gap and then prying open the shell.

**Conservation status**      **Least concern**

# European Herring Gull

*Larus argentatus*

Birds

Game birds and waterbirds

Waterbirds

## Factfile

| | |
|---|---|
| **Habitat** | Coast, estuaries, open ocean, grassland |
| **Distribution** | North and Central America, Europe, Asia |
| **Length** | 22 to 26 in |
| **Weight** | 1.5 to 3.3 lb |
| **Life span** | Up to 30 years |
| **Migration** | Partial migrant |

**Diet** Herring gulls are opportunistic feeders. They eat fish, earthworms, crabs, birds, eggs, rodents and insects. They also scavenge at refuse dumps.

**Fact** Communication between herring gulls is complex and highly developed. They are known to use calls and body language to understand each other.

**Conservation status**      **Least concern**

# Little Auk
*Alle alle*

## Factfile

| | |
|---|---|
| **Habitat** | Coast, shallow sea, open ocean |
| **Distribution** | Arctic |
| **Length** | 7.5 to 9 in |
| **Weight** | 5 to 6 oz |
| **Life span** | 10 to 25 years |
| **Migration** | Migrant |

**Diet** Little auks hunt marine crustaceans by diving to depths of up to 100 feet and then swimming upward in a zigzag pattern to capture their prey.

**Fact** A breeding population of little auks in Greenland is among the largest group of auks. It is believed to include about 30 million birds.

**Conservation status**      **Least concern**

# Greater Flamingo

*Phoenicopterus roseus*

## Factfile

| | |
|---|---|
| **Habitat** | Lakes, coast, estuaries, wetland |
| **Distribution** | Central and South America, Europe, Asia, Africa |
| **Height** | 4 to 5 ft |
| **Weight** | 4.6 to 9 lb |
| **Life span** | Up to 40 years |
| **Migration** | Partial migrant |

**Diet** This bird uses its feet to stir up mud, then sucks water through its bill to filter out shrimp, seeds, algae, microscopic organisms and mollusks.

**Fact** The flamingo's pink color is due to the food it eats. Shrimp and blue-green algae contain carotenoid pigment, which turns their feathers pink.

**Conservation status**      **Least concern**

# Lesser Flamingo
*Phoenicopterus minor*

## Factfile

| | |
|---|---|
| **Habitat** | Lakes, coast, desert, intertidal zones |
| **Distribution** | West, central and southern Africa |
| **Height** | 2.6 to 3.3 ft |
| **Weight** | 2.5 to 6 lb |
| **Life span** | 20 to 30 years |
| **Migration** | Nomadic |

**Diet** Lesser flamingos eat shrimp, snails and algae. They plunge their heads upside down into the water and scoop fish using their upper bills like a shovel.

**Fact** Young flamingos are not pink. They begin life with soft, downy white feathers. As the flamingo matures its feathers will become a pink color.

**Conservation status**      **Near threatened**

# Green Heron

*Butorides virescens*

## Factfile

| | |
|---|---|
| **Habitat** | Lakes, rivers, wetland, swamp, marsh |
| **Distribution** | The Americas |
| **Length** | 16 to 21 in |
| **Weight** | 4.5 to 8 oz |
| **Life span** | Up to 7 years |
| **Migration** | Partial migrant |

**Diet** Green herons feed at the edge of the water eating mostly small fish, some crustaceans, mollusks, insects, reptiles, amphibians and leeches.

**Fact** They communicate with other green herons by using elaborate calls and postures to signal warnings, territorial displays and mating dances.

| **Conservation status** | **Least concern** |
|---|---|

# Grey Heron
*Area cinerea*

## Factfile

**Habitat**       Lakes, rivers, streams, wetland
**Distribution**  Europe, Asia, Africa
**Length**        35 to 40 in
**Weight**        2.2 to 4.5 lb
**Life span**     Up to 5 years
**Migration**     Partial migrant

**Diet**
Grey herons are opportunist feeders. They eat a wide variety of fish, invertebrates, ducklings and land animals, such as rats and young rabbits.

**Fact**
Herons mostly build large colonies of nests in trees. Most of these nests are at least 80 feet above the ground. These colonies are called heronries.

| Conservation status | Least concern |
|---|---|

# Wood Stork

*Mycteria americana*

## Factfile

| | |
|---|---|
| **Habitat** | Rivers, marsh, mangrove, coast |
| **Distribution** | The Americas, Caribbean |
| **Length** | 33 to 45 in |
| **Weight** | Up to 5.8 lb |
| **Life span** | 11 to 18 years |
| **Migration** | Partial migrant |

**Diet** The wood stork feeds during the day and at night. It has a varied diet including small fish, frogs, mollusks, snails, insects and aquatic invertebrates.

**Fact** Wood storks use an unusual method to catch fish. They open their bills underwater, wait patiently for a fish to pass by, then close their bills around it.

**Conservation status**      **Least concern**

# White Stork
*Ciconia ciconia*

## Factfile

| | |
|---|---|
| **Habitat** | Wetland, savannah, meadows, fields |
| **Distribution** | Europe, Africa, Asia |
| **Length** | 39 to 45 in |
| **Weight** | 5 to 9.5 lb |
| **Life span** | Up to 25 years |
| **Migration** | Migrant |

**Diet** The white stork enjoys a varied diet. It feeds on insects, frogs, rodents, lizards and snakes. It will even catch and eat some small birds.

**Fact** White storks build enormous nests that can be as large as 6 feet in diameter and over 9 feet deep. Some storks' nests can even weigh up to a ton!

**Conservation status**  **Least concern**

# Scarlet Ibis

*Eudocimus ruber*

## Factfile

| | |
|---|---|
| **Habitat** | Coast, swamp, wetland |
| **Distribution** | Central and South America |
| **Length** | 22 to 27 in |
| **Weight** | 1.5 to 2.1 lb |
| **Life span** | Up to 20 years |
| **Migration** | Nonmigrant |

**Diet** The scarlet ibis enjoys a varied diet that includes crabs and other crustaceans, small fish, mollusks, earthworms, insects and some amphibians.

**Fact** Natural predators of the scarlet ibis include raccoons, snakes and large cats. Some humans also kill these birds for their beautiful feathers.

**Conservation status**          **Least concern**

60

# African Spoonbill

*Platalea alba*

## Factfile

| | |
|---|---|
| **Habitat** | Wetland, marsh |
| **Distribution** | Africa (south of Sahara), Madagascar |
| **Height** | 2.5 to 3 ft |
| **Weight** | 3 to 4.5 lb |
| **Life span** | Up to 30 years |
| **Migration** | Partial migrant |

**Diet** The African spoonbill eats a diet of aquatic insects and their larvae, mollusks, crustaceans, worms, leeches, small fish, frogs and some plant material.

**Fact** This bird wades through water, sweeping its bill from side to side. Prey is caught in the spoon of the bill and eaten with a toss of the head.

**Conservation status**      **Least concern**

# Great Egret

*Ardea alba*

Birds

Game birds and waterbirds

Waterbirds

## Factfile

| | |
|---|---|
| **Habitat** | Wetland, lakes, marsh, estuaries, swamp |
| **Distribution** | The Americas, Africa, Asia, Australia |
| **Length** | 3 to 3.5 ft |
| **Weight** | Up to 2.2 lb |
| **Life span** | Up to 15 years |
| **Migration** | Partial migrant |

**Diet** Great egrets mainly eat small fish but also amphibians, reptiles, birds, small mammals and invertebrates, such as crayfish, prawns and worms.

**Fact** Great egrets fly slowly but powerfully. They use just two wing beats per second to achieve their cruising speed of around 35 miles per hour.

| Conservation status | Least concern |
|---|---|

# Shoebill

*Balaeniceps rex*

## Factfile

| | |
|---|---|
| **Habitat** | Marsh, swamp, wetland |
| **Distribution** | Central Africa |
| **Height** | 3.6 to 4.6 ft |
| **Weight** | 10 to 14 lb |
| **Life span** | Up to 35 years |
| **Migration** | Nonmigrant |

**Diet** Shoebills eat lungfish, bichirs, catfish, tilapia and water snakes. They will also eat frogs, young crocodiles, lizards, turtles, mollusks and some carrion.

**Fact** Despite weighing as much as 14 lb, shoebills are often found perched on floating vegetation from where they do their fishing.

**Conservation status**        **Vulnerable**

# Grey Crowned Crane

*Balearica regulorum*

## Factfile

| | |
|---|---|
| **Habitat** | Wetland, grassland |
| **Distribution** | East and South Africa |
| **Length** | 3.2 to 3.6 ft |
| **Weight** | 6.6 to 8.8 lb |
| **Life span** | Up to 22 years |
| **Migration** | Nonmigrant |

**Diet** The grey crowned crane has a diet of grasses, seeds, insects and other invertebrates, small vertebrates, groundnuts, soybeans, maize and millet.

**Fact** This crane's booming call involves inflating the red throat skin. It also makes a honking sound quite different from the trumpeting of other cranes.

**Conservation status**          **Vulnerable**

# Common Crane

*Grus grus*

## Factfile

| | |
|---|---|
| **Habitat** | Estuaries, lakes, forest, wetland, grassland |
| **Distribution** | Europe, Asia, North Africa |
| **Length** | 3.2 to 4.2 ft |
| **Weight** | 11 to 13 lb |
| **Life span** | Up to 13 years |
| **Migration** | Migrant |

**Diet** The common crane's diet contains mostly plants, seeds, cereals, roots and stems. It will also feed on some insects, mollusks and small crustaceans.

**Fact** The common crane flies higher than any other crane species. It has been recorded flying at impressive altitudes of approximately 3000 feet.

**Conservation status**      Least concern

65

# Atlantic Puffin

*Fratercula arctica*

## Factfile

| | |
|---|---|
| **Habitat** | Coast, shallow sea, open ocean |
| **Distribution** | North Atlantic, Arctic Ocean |
| **Length** | 11 to 12 in |
| **Weight** | 12 to 16 oz |
| **Life span** | Up to 20 years |
| **Migration** | Migrant |

**Diet** The Atlantic puffin's diet consists of fish such as herring, hake, capelin and sand lance. They will also occasionally eat mollusks and crustaceans.

**Fact** At 45 days old the Atlantic puffin chick leaves its burrow and spends the next 3–5 years at sea learning about feeding places and choosing a mate.

| Conservation status | Least concern |
|---|---|

# Wandering Albatross

**Diomedea exulans**

## Factfile

| | |
|---|---|
| **Habitat** | Open ocean, but nests on ridges and hillocks |
| **Distribution** | Antarctica |
| **Length** | 3.6 to 4.5 ft |
| **Weight** | 14 to 26 lb |
| **Life span** | Up to 50 years |
| **Migration** | Migrant |

**Diet** The wandering albatross's diet includes fish, jellyfish, cephalopods and occasionally crustaceans. They also eat penguin and seal carrion.

**Fact** Young wandering albatrosses remain at sea for 5 to 10 years before returning to the island where they were raised in order to breed.

**Conservation status**      **Vulnerable**

# Southern Giant Petrel

*Macronectes giganteus*

## Factfile

| | |
|---|---|
| **Habitat** | Open ocean, but nests in colonies on islands |
| **Distribution** | Antarctica |
| **Length** | 2.8 to 3.3 ft |
| **Weight** | 7 to 17 lb |
| **Life span** | Up to 25 years |
| **Migration** | Migrant |

**Diet** The southern giant petrel is a scavenger. It typically feeds on scraps of partially devoured seal pups or seabirds discarded by other predators.

**Fact** When threatened, the southern giant petrel warns off potential attackers with loud calls. It will also spit out foul-smelling stomach oil.

**Conservation status**      **Least concern**

# Snow Petrel

*Pagodroma nivea*

## Factfile

| | |
|---|---|
| **Habitat** | Open water, but nests on cliffs and rock faces |
| **Distribution** | Antarctica |
| **Length** | 12 to 16 in |
| **Weight** | 9 to 16 oz |
| **Life span** | 11 to 14 years |
| **Migration** | Migrant |

**Diet** Snow petrels eat mainly fish, squid and other mollusks, and krill. They also feed on the carcasses of dead seals, whales and penguins.

**Fact** The snow petrel builds its nest in the rock of cliff faces. The birds seal the nests off with snow that is glued in place with saliva.

**Conservation status**     **Least concern**

69

# Great Crested Grebe

*Podiceps cristatus*

## Factfile

| | |
|---|---|
| **Habitat** | Lakes, coast, estuaries |
| **Distribution** | Europe, Asia, Africa, Australia, New Zealand |
| **Length** | 18 to 20 in |
| **Weight** | 1.3 to 3.3 lb |
| **Life span** | Up to 11 years |
| **Migration** | Partial migrant |

**Diet** Great crested grebes feed on fish of various sizes and species. They also eat insects, crustaceans, mollusks and occasionally some amphibians.

**Fact** They are known for their courtship displays, where pairs raise and shake their heads and approach each other with weed in their bills.

| Conservation status | Least concern |
|---|---|

# Black-eared Grebe

*Podiceps nigricollis*

## Factfile

| | |
|---|---|
| **Habitat** | Lakes, coast, estuaries, wetland |
| **Distribution** | North America, Europe, Asia, Africa |
| **Length** | 11.8 to 13.8 in |
| **Weight** | 9 to 22 oz |
| **Life span** | Up to 7 years |
| **Migration** | Migrant |

**Diet** Crustaceans and insects make up the majority of the black-eared grebe's diet, but brine shrimp are also eaten in salty lake habitats.

**Fact** Black-eared grebes are almost flightless for around nine months of each year. They are not good flyers and will almost only ever fly when migrating.

**Conservation status**  **Least concern**

# Western Grebe

*Aechmophorus occidentalis*

## Factfile

| | |
|---|---|
| **Habitat** | Lakes, marsh, coast, estuaries |
| **Distribution** | North America |
| **Length** | 22 to 29 in |
| **Weight** | 2.2 to 4.4 lb |
| **Life span** | Up to 14 years |
| **Migration** | Migrant |

**Diet** Western grebes eat mainly fish, diving in open water to catch them. They also occasionally consume bottom-dwelling crustaceans and worms.

**Fact** The western grebe, like other grebes, spends most of its time in water. Its legs are so far back on its body that walking is very difficult.

| **Conservation status** | **Least concern** |
|---|---|

# Osprey
## *Pandion haliaetus*

## Factfile

| | |
|---|---|
| **Habitat** | Coast, estuaries, lakes, marsh, rivers, swamp |
| **Distribution** | Worldwide (except Antarctica) |
| **Length** | 21 to 26 in |
| **Weight** | 3.3 to 4.4 lb |
| **Life span** | Up to 20 years |
| **Migration** | Migrant |

**Diet** The osprey has a diet made up almost exclusively of fish. They catch their food by plunging feetfirst into the water straight from the air.

**Fact** Barbed pads on the soles of the birds' feet help them grip slippery fish. They carry fish headfirst when flying which reduces wind resistance.

| **Conservation status** | **Least concern** |
|---|---|

# Harpy Eagle
## *Harpia harpyja*

Birds

**Birds of prey**

**Diurnal birds of prey**

## Factfile

| | |
|---|---|
| **Habitat** | Rain forest |
| **Distribution** | Southern Mexico to central South America |
| **Length** | 3 to 3.3 ft |
| **Weight** | 10 to 20 lb |
| **Life span** | 25 to 35 years |
| **Migration** | Nonmigrant |

**Diet** The harpy eagle preys primarily on tree-dwelling mammals such as sloths, monkeys and opossums. They occasionally eat reptiles and other birds.

**Fact** The harpy eagle is classed as one of the world's apex predators. This means that, as an adult, it has no natural predators within its ecosystem.

| Conservation status | Near threatened |
|---|---|

# Golden Eagle

*Aquila chrysaetos*

## Factfile

| | |
|---|---|
| **Habitat** | Desert, forest, grassland, moorland, taiga |
| **Distribution** | North America, Europe, Asia, North Africa |
| **Length** | 2.5 to 3 ft |
| **Weight** | 7 to 14 lb |
| **Life span** | 20 to 40 years |
| **Migration** | Partial migrant |

**Diet** Golden eagles mostly eat small mammals such as marmots, rabbits and squirrels. They also eat carrion, reptiles, birds, fish and large insects.

**Fact** Golden eagles often hunt in pairs. One will chase the prey until it shows signs of exhaustion, then the other eagle will swoop down and seize it.

**Conservation status**          **Least concern**

75

# Bald Eagle

*Haliaeetus leucocephalus*

Birds

Birds of prey

Diurnal birds of prey

## Factfile

| | |
|---|---|
| **Habitat** | Desert, grassland, forest, mountains |
| **Distribution** | North America |
| **Length** | 2.5 to 3.5 ft |
| **Weight** | 6.5 to 14 lb |
| **Life span** | Up to 28 years |
| **Migration** | Partial migrant |

**Diet** Bald eagles eat mainly fish, including salmon, herring and catfish. They will also feed on birds, reptiles, amphibians, invertebrates and mammals.

**Fact** Bald eagles often steal other creatures' catches. They will harass a hunting osprey until the smaller bird drops its prey and the eagle catches it.

**Conservation status**      **Least concern**

# Northern Goshawk

*Accipiter gentilis*

## Factfile

| | |
|---|---|
| **Habitat** | Forest, taiga, grassland |
| **Distribution** | Canada to Mexico, Europe, Asia |
| **Length** | 20 to 26 in |
| **Weight** | 2.2 to 3.3 lb |
| **Life span** | Up to 11 years |
| **Migration** | Partial migrant |

**Diet** The bulk of this bird's diet is made up of small mammals and birds found in forests, such as pigeons, gulls, squirrels, mice, rabbits and hares.

**Fact** Northern goshawks are well known for fiercely defending their nests. They will attack people and animals that get too close.

| Conservation status | Least concern |
|---|---|

# Red Kite
*Milvus milvus*

## Factfile

| | |
|---|---|
| **Habitat** | Forest, desert, grassland, wetland |
| **Distribution** | Europe, west Asia, North Africa |
| **Length** | 23 to 26 in |
| **Weight** | 1.6 to 2.2 lb |
| **Life span** | 4 to 5 years |
| **Migration** | Partial migrant |

**Diet** The red kite mainly eats small mammals such as mice, voles, shrews, young hares and rabbits. It will also feed on a wide variety of carrion.

**Fact** Some red kites have been known to decorate their nests with paper, plastic and other man-made materials, even stealing clothes left out to dry!

| **Conservation status** | **Near threatened** |
|---|---|

# Common Buzzard
*Buteo buteo*

## Factfile

| | |
|---|---|
| **Habitat** | Woodland, forest, grassland, mountains |
| **Distribution** | Europe, Asia, Africa |
| **Length** | 18 to 24 in |
| **Weight** | 1.1 to 2.2 lb |
| **Life span** | Up to 8 years |
| **Migration** | Partial migrant |

**Diet** Common buzzards have a wide-ranging diet including mammals such as rabbits, hares and squirrels. They will also eat other birds and carrion.

**Fact** During the breeding season, buzzards perform spectacular aerial displays, circling high in the sky before tumbling down towards the ground.

**Conservation status**  **Least concern**

# Peregrine Falcon

*Falco peregrinus*

## Factfile

| | |
|---|---|
| **Habitat** | Coast, forest, desert, grassland, heathland |
| **Distribution** | Worldwide (except Antarctica) |
| **Length** | 14 to 19 in |
| **Weight** | 1.1 to 3.3 lb |
| **Life span** | Up to 17 years |
| **Migration** | Partial migrant |

**Diet** Peregrine falcons eat medium-sized birds such as pigeons, waterfowl and waders. They sometimes eat small mammals, fish, insects and reptiles too.

**Fact** Peregrine falcons are fearsome hunters. They dive at speeds of over 200 miles per hour to grab their prey in midair with their strong talons.

| **Conservation status** | **Least concern** |
|---|---|

# Turkey Vulture
*Cathartes aura*

## Factfile

| | |
|---|---|
| **Habitat** | Forest, coast, desert, plains |
| **Distribution** | From southern Canada to South America |
| **Length** | 25 to 32 in |
| **Weight** | 2 to 4.5 lb |
| **Life span** | Up to 16 years |
| **Migration** | Partial migrant |

**Diet** Turkey vultures eat carrion, which they find largely by using their excellent sense of smell. These vultures almost never attack living prey.

**Fact** The word vulture comes from the Latin *vellere*, which means to pluck or tear. They were named for the way that they feast on dead animals.

**Conservation status**        **Least concern**

# Barn Owl

*Tyto alba*

## Factfile

| | |
|---|---|
| **Habitat** | Grassland, moorland |
| **Distribution** | The Americas, Europe, Asia, Africa, Australia |
| **Length** | 12 to 18 in |
| **Weight** | 12 to 24 oz |
| **Life span** | 1 to 2 years |
| **Migration** | Nonmigrant |

**Diet** Barn owls eat small mammals such as voles, shrews and mice. Prey is swallowed whole and indigestible parts are later coughed up as a pellet.

**Fact** Barn owls hunt during the dark of night. Although they have very good eyesight, they rely mostly on their acute sense of hearing to find prey.

**Conservation status**     Least concern

# Snowy Owl
## *Bubo scandiacus*

## Factfile

| | |
|---|---|
| **Habitat** | Tundra |
| **Distribution** | Arctic |
| **Length** | 21 to 28 in |
| **Weight** | 2.5 to 5.5 lb |
| **Life span** | 9 to 10 years |
| **Migration** | Partial migrant |

**Diet** The snowy owl's favorite food is lemming – a small mouse-like rodent – but they also hunt for other small rodents, rabbits, birds and fish.

**Fact** Unlike most owls, which are purely nocturnal, the snowy owl has adapted so it is active and can hunt both during the day and at night.

**Conservation status**          **Least concern**

# Great Horned Owl

*Bubo virginianus*

Birds

Birds of prey

Nocturnal birds of prey

## Factfile

| | |
|---|---|
| **Habitat** | Forest, woodland, desert, urban areas |
| **Distribution** | The Americas |
| **Length** | 18 to 24 in |
| **Weight** | 1.75 to 5.5 lb |
| **Life span** | 5 to 15 years |
| **Migration** | Nonmigrant |

**Diet** This owl's prey ranges from tiny rodents and scorpions to hares, skunks, geese and other birds of prey. They will also eat fish, insects and carrion.

**Fact** Using their powerful and sharp talons, great horned owls are able to kill and then carry animals several times heavier than themselves.

**Conservation status** **Least concern**

# Tawny Owl
*Strix aluco*

## Factfile

| | |
|---|---|
| **Habitat** | Forest, parkland, urban areas |
| **Distribution** | Europe, Asia, northwest Africa |
| **Length** | 14.5 to 15.5 in |
| **Weight** | 16 to 19 oz |
| **Life span** | Up to 5 years |
| **Migration** | Nonmigrant |

**Diet** This nocturnal bird of prey hunts mainly rodents, usually by dropping from a perch to seize its prey. In urban areas they will often eat birds.

**Fact** Tawny owls are specially adapted for hunting in woodland. They have short wings, which allow them to maneuver easily between trees.

**Conservation status**     **Least concern**

85

# European Nightjar

*Caprimulgus europaeus*

## Factfile

| | |
|---|---|
| **Habitat** | Heathland, woodland, wetland |
| **Distribution** | Europe, Asia, Africa |
| **Length** | 9.5 to 11 in |
| **Weight** | 1.8 to 3.6 oz |
| **Life span** | Up to 4 years |
| **Migration** | Migrant |

**Diet** The European nightjar eats insects, especially moths and beetles. They largely feed at dawn and dusk, when insects are most active.

**Fact** European nightjar are able to demonstrate amazing aerial agility as they execute rapid twists and turns in pursuit of their prey.

**Conservation status**     **Least concern**

86

# Tawny Frogmouth
## *Podargus strigoides*

## Factfile

| | |
|---|---|
| **Habitat** | Forest, woodland, parkland |
| **Distribution** | New Guinea, Australia |
| **Length** | 13 to 21 in |
| **Weight** | Up to 1.5 lb |
| **Life span** | Up to 10 years |
| **Migration** | Nonmigrant |

**Diet** The diet of the tawny frogmouth includes a variety of insects as well as spiders, worms, slugs and snails, small mammals, reptiles, frogs and some birds.

**Fact** During the day they usually sleep in a sedentary position. When disturbed they raise their head and stiffen their body, simulating a branch.

**Conservation status**     Least concern

87

# Eastern Kingbird
*Tyrannus tyrannus*

## Factfile

| | |
|---|---|
| **Habitat** | Grassland, parkland, lakes, forest |
| **Distribution** | The Americas |
| **Length** | 7.5 to 9.5 in |
| **Weight** | 1.2 to 1.9 oz |
| **Life span** | Up to 7 years |
| **Migration** | Migrant |

**Diet**
Eastern kingbirds mostly eat insects such as bees, wasps, ants, beetles, crickets, locusts, grasshoppers and flies. They will also eat some fruit.

**Fact**
When migrating they fly during the day in flocks of up to 60 birds. They will join much larger flocks to travel across substantial bodies of water.

| **Conservation status** | **Least concern** |
|---|---|

# Superb Fairy-wren

*Malurus cyaneus*

## Factfile

| | |
|---|---|
| **Habitat** | Woodland, urban areas |
| **Distribution** | Australia, New Guinea |
| **Length** | 5.5 to 6.5 in |
| **Weight** | .3 to .45 oz |
| **Life span** | Up to 10 years |
| **Migration** | Nonmigrant |

**Diet** Superb fairy-wrens feed on insects and invertebrates. These are generally caught on the ground, but may also be taken from low bushes.

**Fact** Wrens have relatively weak powers of flight, so they spend most of their time hopping on the ground or in shrubs, while they gather their food.

**Conservation status**      **Least concern**

# Japanese Waxwing

*Bombycilla japonica*

## Factfile

| | |
|---|---|
| **Habitat** | Forest, parkland, urban areas |
| **Distribution** | Asia, Europe |
| **Length** | 6 to 7 in |
| **Weight** | 1 to 1.2 oz |
| **Life span** | Up to 8 years |
| **Migration** | Migrant |

**Diet** The Japanese waxwing feeds on berries and insects during the breeding season. Outside this period, it eats various fruit and berries.

**Fact** They breed in forests in the Russian Far East and northeast China. Japanese waxwings are at risk of becoming threatened due to loss of their forest habitat.

| Conservation status | Near threatened |
|---|---|

# New Zealand Fantail

*Rhipidura fuliginosa*

## Factfile

| | |
|---|---|
| **Habitat** | Forest, urban areas |
| **Distribution** | New Zealand |
| **Length** | 5.5 to 7.5 in |
| **Weight** | .3 to .4 oz |
| **Life span** | Up to 3 years |
| **Migration** | Nonmigrant |

**Diet** The fantail's diet is mainly insects, usually caught in midair. With its "fan tail" it can change direction very quickly to capture insects in flight.

**Fact** Fantails do not live for long, so it is very important that they have lots of babies to keep the species going. They can have up to four clutches a year.

| **Conservation status** | **Least concern** |
|---|---|

# Blue Jay
## *Cyanocitta cristata*

## Factfile

| | |
|---|---|
| **Habitat** | Forest, urban areas |
| **Distribution** | North America |
| **Length** | 10 to 12 in |
| **Weight** | 2.5 to 3.5 oz |
| **Life span** | 7 to 8 years |
| **Migration** | Migrant |

**Diet** Blue jays glean insects and feed on nuts and seeds in trees, shrubs, and on the ground. They also eat grains and sometimes raid other nests for eggs.

**Fact** The black markings across the face, nape and throat vary extensively and it is believed that this may help blue jays recognize one another.

**Conservation status**  **Least concern**

# Northern Raven
*Corvus corax*

## Factfile

**Habitat**        Forest, coast, desert, grassland, tundra
**Distribution**   North America, Europe, Africa, Asia
**Length**         24 to 26 in
**Weight**         1.5 to 4.4 lb
**Life span**      10 to 15 years
**Migration**      Nonmigrant

**Diet**   Northern ravens eat almost anything they can get hold of, from carrion, small mammals, other birds, eggs, insects and fish, to wolf and dog dung!

**Fact**   These birds are acrobatic fliers, who perform rolls and somersaults. They have even been recorded flying upside down for more than half a mile.

**Conservation status**        **Least concern**

# Great Tit
*Parus major*

## Factfile

| | |
|---|---|
| **Habitat** | Woodland, urban areas |
| **Distribution** | Europe, Asia, North Africa, the Middle East |
| **Length** | 5 to 5.5 in |
| **Weight** | .5 to .75 oz |
| **Life span** | Up to 3 years |
| **Migration** | Nonmigrant |

**Diet** Great tits feed on invertebrates and insects, and some berries and seeds. During the breeding season, they prefer to eat protein-rich caterpillars.

**Fact** Great tits are very happy to live close to humans. They often use nest boxes in gardens and have even been known to nest inside mailboxes.

**Conservation status**     **Least concern**

# Eurasian Wren
### *Troglodytes hiemalis*

## Factfile

| | |
|---|---|
| **Habitat** | Woodland, cliff faces, riparian areas |
| **Distribution** | North America |
| **Length** | 3 to 4.8 in |
| **Weight** | .3 to .4 oz |
| **Life span** | Up to 7 years |
| **Migration** | Migrant |

**Diet** The Eurasian wren's diet is mostly made up of insects and invertebrates. It survives rough winters by foraging for insects in bark and rotting wood.

**Fact** The male Eurasian wren builds many stick nests in crevices and other nooks. The female chooses the one she wants, and lines it with soft material.

**Conservation status**     **Least concern**

95

# European Robin

*Erithacus rubecula*

## Factfile

| | |
|---|---|
| **Habitat** | Woodland, urban areas |
| **Distribution** | Europe, Asia |
| **Length** | 5 to 5.5 in |
| **Weight** | .5 to .7 oz |
| **Life span** | Up to 1 year |
| **Migration** | Partial migrant |

**Diet** European robins mostly eat insects and worms, which are caught by snatching the prey on the ground after watching for movement from a perch above.

**Fact** European robins are territorial and will fight other robins who venture into their territory. Sometimes they will even fight to the death.

**Conservation status**      **Least concern**

# House Sparrow

*Passer domesticus*

## Factfile

| | |
|---|---|
| **Habitat** | Farmland, parkland, urban areas |
| **Distribution** | Worldwide (excluding polar regions) |
| **Length** | 5.9 to 6.7 in |
| **Weight** | .95 to 1 oz |
| **Life span** | 1 to 4 years |
| **Migration** | Nonmigrant |

**Diet** House sparrows eat mostly grains and seeds, as well as livestock feed. In urban areas they will eat discarded food. In summer they eat insects.

**Fact** House sparrows prefer to nest in man-made structures such as walls and nest boxes, instead of in natural nest sites such as holes in trees.

**Conservation status**     **Least concern**

97

# Java Sparrow

*Padda oryzivora*

## Factfile

| | |
|---|---|
| **Habitat** | Woodland, mangrove, grassland |
| **Distribution** | Indonesia, Asia, Australia, Tanzania |
| **Length** | 5.9 to 6.7 in |
| **Weight** | .7 to 1 oz |
| **Life span** | 5 to 9 years |
| **Migration** | Nonmigrant |

**Diet** Java sparrows are known for eating rice. They can cause huge damage to crops. They will also feed on nuts, seeds and other grains.

**Fact** Java sparrows originally came from Java but they have been introduced all over the world as a consequence of their popularity as pets.

**Conservation status**     **Vulnerable**

# Northern Cardinal

*Cardinalis cardinalis*

## Factfile

| | |
|---|---|
| **Habitat** | Forest, woodland, parkland |
| **Distribution** | North America |
| **Length** | 8.3 to 9.1 in |
| **Weight** | 1.5 to 1.7 oz |
| **Life span** | Up to 15 years |
| **Migration** | Nonmigrant |

**Diet** Northern cardinals eat a diet mostly consisting of seeds and fruit, but they will supplement their diet with insects for extra protein.

**Fact** The female northern cardinal is one of a very few female North American songbirds that actually sing. She does this while sitting on the nest.

**Conservation status**   Least concern

# Painted Bunting

*Passerina ciris*

Birds

Perching birds and relatives

Perching birds

## Factfile

| | |
|---|---|
| **Habitat** | Savannah, grassland, scrub forest |
| **Distribution** | The Americas |
| **Length** | 4.5 to 5.1 in |
| **Weight** | .5 to .7 oz |
| **Life span** | Up to 10 years |
| **Migration** | Migrant |

**Diet**  Painted buntings eat seeds and insects. They eat mostly insects during the mating season. These birds forage on the ground or in low brush.

**Fact**  Male birds are aggressive and territorial, even killing intruding birds in some cases. Threat displays include pecking and flapping.

**Conservation status**    Near threatened

# African Grey Parrot

*Psittacus erithacus*

## Factfile

| | |
|---|---|
| **Habitat** | Rain forest |
| **Distribution** | West to central Africa |
| **Length** | 12.5 to 14 in |
| **Weight** | 14 to 17 oz |
| **Life span** | 30 to 40 years |
| **Migration** | Nonmigrant |

**Diet** African grey parrots climb through tree branches collecting seeds, nuts, fruit and berries. They particularly enjoy the outer layer of the oil palm nut.

**Fact** The African grey parrot can fluff up its feathers so it looks much bigger than it really is. It will do this to defend itself from any predators.

**Conservation status**     **Near threatened**

# Red-and-green Macaw
*Ara chloropterus*

Birds

Perching birds and relatives

Parrots

## Factfile

| | |
|---|---|
| **Habitat** | Forest and rain forest |
| **Distribution** | North and central South America |
| **Length** | 35 to 37 in |
| **Weight** | 2.8 to 3.8 lb |
| **Life span** | 40 to 50 years |
| **Migration** | Nonmigrant |

**Diet** Macaws eat fruit and nuts, especially Brazil nuts. In addition they will gnaw at the bark of deciduous trees in order to absorb fibers and vitamins.

**Fact** In the wild, macaws often flock to mountains of clay known as "macaw licks." Such licks contain minerals and salts essential to the bird's diet.

| Conservation status | Least concern |
|---|---|

# Rainbow Lorikeet

*Trichoglossus haematodus*

## Factfile

| | |
|---|---|
| **Habitat** | Rain forest, forest, heathland, mangrove |
| **Distribution** | Southeast Asia, southwest Pacific Islands, Australia |
| **Length** | 9.8 to 11.8 in |
| **Weight** | 2.6 to 5.6 oz |
| **Life span** | Up to 20 years |
| **Migration** | Nonmigrant |

**Diet** Rainbow lorikeets have a diet made up of flowers, pollen, nectar, seeds, insects and some fruit. These colorful birds feed while upside down!

**Fact** Rainbow lorikeets are very noisy birds. They give out sharp, screeching calls when flying, and continue with their shrill chatters while eating.

**Conservation status**          **Least concern**

# Sulphur-crested Cockatoo

## *Cacatua galerita*

## Factfile

| | |
|---|---|
| **Habitat** | Forest, grassland, urban areas |
| **Distribution** | New Guinea, Australia |
| **Length** | 18 to 20 in |
| **Weight** | 1.5 to 2 lb |
| **Life span** | Up to 40 years |
| **Migration** | Nonmigrant |

**Diet** Sulphur-crested cockatoos eat berries, seeds, nuts and roots. Feeding takes place in groups, with some birds watching for danger from a nearby perch.

**Fact** These birds are very noisy. They will often produce a loud, shrill cry. Cockatoos can mimic the sounds of other animals, including people!

**Conservation status**     Least concern

# Galah
### *Eolophus roseicapilla*

## Factfile

| | |
|---|---|
| **Habitat** | Woodland, scrubland, grassland, urban areas |
| **Distribution** | Australia |
| **Length** | 12 to 14 in |
| **Weight** | 9.5 to 12.5 oz |
| **Life span** | Up to 40 years |
| **Migration** | Nonmigrant |

**Diet** Galahs typically feed on the ground, where they eat a range of seeds, from cereals to grasses. They also eat berries, buds, flowers and insect larvae.

**Fact** Galahs are thought of as playful birds. They enjoy doing spins and aerobatics when flying, and hanging upside down when they land in trees.

| **Conservation status** | **Least concern** |
|---|---|

# Common Cuckoo
*Cuculus canorus*

Birds

Perching birds and relatives

Cuckoos and turacos

## Factfile

| | |
|---|---|
| **Habitat** | Forest, farmland, grassland, wetland |
| **Distribution** | Europe, Asia, Africa |
| **Length** | 12 to 14 in |
| **Weight** | 3.8 to 4.4 oz |
| **Life span** | Up to 12 years |
| **Migration** | Migrant |

**Diet** The common cuckoo's diet consists of invertebrates, especially hairy caterpillars, beetles, spiders, centipedes, earthworms and insect larvae.

**Fact** The common cuckoo is the only member of the cuckoo family that calls "cuckoo-cuckoo-cuckoo." Others have loud voices but different-sounding calls.

**Conservation status**     **Least concern**

# Greater Roadrunner
## *Geococcyx californianus*

## Factfile

| | |
|---|---|
| **Habitat** | Desert, grassland and woodland |
| **Distribution** | North America |
| **Length** | 20 to 24 in |
| **Weight** | 8 to 12 oz |
| **Life span** | 7 to 8 years |
| **Migration** | Nonmigrant |

**Diet** Greater roadrunners eat small snakes, lizards, scorpions, mice, spiders, ground-nesting birds and insects. They will also eat fruit and seeds.

**Fact** The greater roadrunner holds its head and tail flat and parallel to the ground when running. It can reach speeds of over 18 miles per hour.

| Conservation status | Least concern |
|---|---|

# Red-crested Turaco
*Tauraco erythrolophus*

## Factfile

| | |
|---|---|
| **Habitat** | Woodland, savannah |
| **Distribution** | Southwest Africa |
| **Length** | 15.8 to 17 in |
| **Weight** | 7 to 11.5 oz |
| **Life span** | 5 to 9 years |
| **Migration** | Nonmigrant |

**Diet** The turaco has a varied diet. They are omnivorous so feed on plant material like fruit, nuts, seeds and berries, as well as animals like invertebrates.

**Fact** The call of a turaco sounds like they are saying "g'way." This is the reason that they have been given the nickname the go-away birds.

**Conservation status**      **Least concern**

# Ruby-throated Hummingbird

*Archilochus colubris*

## Factfile

| | |
|---|---|
| **Habitat** | Forest, urban areas |
| **Distribution** | North America to Central America |
| **Length** | 3 to 4 in |
| **Weight** | .08 to .21 oz |
| **Life span** | 3 to 5 years |
| **Migration** | Migrant |

**Diet** These birds feed on the nectar of flowers such as trumpet creeper, honeysuckle and bee balm. They supplement this diet with some insects.

**Fact** Ruby-throated hummingbirds prefer to feed from red or orange flowers. Like many other birds, they have amazing color vision.

**Conservation status**     **Least concern**

109

# Sword-billed Hummingbird

*Ensifera ensifera*

Birds

Perching birds and relatives

Hummingbirds and swifts

## Factfile

| | |
|---|---|
| **Habitat** | Forest, woodland |
| **Distribution** | South America (the Andes) |
| **Length** | 6.5 to 9 in |
| **Weight** | .42 to .53 oz |
| **Life span** | 3 to 12 years |
| **Migration** | Nonmigrant |

**Diet** These birds use their long, straw-like tongues to retrieve the nectar from flowers. They also eat some small spiders and insects for added protein.

**Fact** The upper plumage is mostly a glittery green. The lower plumage is lighter in the male and white with greenish-black spots in the female.

**Conservation status**      Least concern

# Common Swift

*Apus apus*

## Factfile

| | |
|---|---|
| **Habitat** | Farmland, parkland, forest, urban areas |
| **Distribution** | Africa, Europe |
| **Length** | 6.3 to 6.7 in |
| **Weight** | 1.2 to 1.7 oz |
| **Life span** | Up to 21 years |
| **Migration** | Migrant |

**Diet** The common swift is insectivorous, feeding on a variety of spiders and flying insects. It gathers most prey in its mouth as it flies through the air.

**Fact** Within 2 days of leaving its nest in Europe, a young swift can be hundreds of miles southward on its first trip to central Africa.

**Conservation status**     **Least concern**

# Great Hornbill

*Buceros bicornis*

Birds

Perching birds and relatives

Hornbills and trogons

## Factfile

| | |
|---|---|
| **Habitat** | Forest, mountains |
| **Distribution** | South and Southeast Asia |
| **Length** | 3.1 to 4 ft |
| **Weight** | 5.5 to 6.6 lb |
| **Life span** | 35 to 40 years |
| **Migration** | Nonmigrant |

**Diet** Fruit is by far the favorite food of great hornbills, though they have also been observed eating snakes, lizards, small rodents and large insects.

**Fact** The horn (called a casque) on the top of the great hornbill's head acts as a "resonating chamber," which amplifies the nasal sound the bird makes.

**Conservation status**    **Near threatened**

# Violaceous Trogon
### *Trogon violaceus*

## Factfile

| | |
|---|---|
| **Habitat** | Forest |
| **Distribution** | Mexico to South America |
| **Length** | 9 to 10.2 in |
| **Weight** | 1.6 to 2.3 oz |
| **Life span** | Unknown |
| **Migration** | Nonmigrant |

**Diet** Violaceous trogons feed on insects and small fruit. They have broad bills and weak legs, which is a reflection of their diet and tree-dwelling life.

**Fact** They often build a nest inside a wasp nest, termite hill, or ant nest. It is believed that this offers some protection and insulation for their eggs.

**Conservation status**  **Least concern**

113

# Resplendent Quetzal

*Pharomachrus mocinno*

## Factfile

| | |
|---|---|
| **Habitat** | Forest |
| **Distribution** | Central America |
| **Length** | 15 to 16 in |
| **Weight** | 7 to 8 oz |
| **Life span** | Unknown |
| **Migration** | Nonmigrant |

**Diet** This bird's favorite foods are fruit from the avocado family. They also feed on insects and some small vertebrates such as lizards and frogs.

**Fact** The resplendent quetzal is not a strong flyer. It can only fly short distances from one tree to another in order to find food and shelter.

**Conservation status**      Near threatened

# Great Spotted Woodpecker

*Dendrocopos major*

## Factfile

| | |
|---|---|
| **Habitat** | Forest |
| **Distribution** | Europe, Asia, North Africa |
| **Length** | 9 to 10 in |
| **Weight** | 2.3 to 3.5 oz |
| **Life span** | Up to 10 years |
| **Migration** | Nonmigrant |

**Diet** In spring and summer these woodpeckers eat insects and the eggs and chicks of hole-nesting birds. Other times they eat fruit, seeds and nuts.

**Fact** Their eggs are white, glossy and about .7 by 1 inch. Male and female birds share the duty of incubating the eggs and feeding the young.

**Conservation status**   Least concern

# Acorn Woodpecker

*Melanerpes formicivorus*

Birds

Perching birds and relatives

Woodpeckers and kingfishers

## Factfile

| | |
|---|---|
| **Habitat** | Forest, woodland, urban areas |
| **Distribution** | The Americas |
| **Length** | 7.5 to 9.1 in |
| **Weight** | 2.3 to 3.2 oz |
| **Life span** | Up to 10 years |
| **Migration** | Nonmigrant |

**Diet** The main diet of the acorn woodpecker consists of insects, sap, oak catkins, fruit, and flower nectar. Acorns are critical for winter survival.

**Fact** They store nuts in individually drilled holes in trees called granaries. The acorns are jammed in so tight that even squirrels can't pry them out!

**Conservation status**      **Least concern**

# Common Kingfisher
### *Alcedo atthis*

## Factfile

| | |
|---|---|
| **Habitat** | Grassland, lakes, forest, rivers |
| **Distribution** | Europe, Asia, North Africa |
| **Length** | 5.9 to 7 in |
| **Weight** | .92 to 1.4 oz |
| **Life span** | 5 to 7 years |
| **Migration** | Partial migrant |

**Diet** Common kingfishers always live close to rivers and streams so that they are able to find small fish, aquatic invertebrates and amphibians to eat.

**Fact** When a kingfisher snatches a fish from the water, it will fly to a nearby tree and beat the fish against the tree, before swallowing it head first.

**Conservation status**      **Least concern**

# Pied Kingfisher

*Ceryle rudis*

## Factfile

| | |
|---|---|
| **Habitat** | Desert, estuaries, forest lakes, sea, rivers |
| **Distribution** | Africa, Asia |
| **Length** | 9.8 to 11.4 in |
| **Weight** | 2.5 to 3.5 oz |
| **Life span** | Up to 3 years |
| **Migration** | Nonmigrant |

**Diet** Pied kingfishers have a diet primarily made up of fish. Unlike other kingfishers, the pied kingfishers swallow their fish during flight.

**Fact** Pied kingfishers are sometimes kept as pets in Nigeria. They are said to be become quite tame after living for just one week in captivity.

| Conservation status | Least concern |
|---|---|

# Laughing Kookaburra

*Dacelo novaeguineae*

## Factfile

| | |
|---|---|
| **Habitat** | Forest, woodland |
| **Distribution** | Australia, New Zealand |
| **Length** | 16.5 to 18.1 in |
| **Weight** | 12 to 15 oz |
| **Life span** | Up to 12 years |
| **Migration** | Nonmigrant |

**Diet** Kookaburras live mainly on a diet of various insects and other invertebrates, but also eat snakes, lizards, rodents and the occasional small bird.

**Fact** The loud voice of the laughing kookaburra can be heard at dawn and dusk. They sound like a variety of trills, chortles, belly laughs and hoots.

**Conservation status**      **Least concern**

# Emerald Toucanet

*Aulacorhynchus prasinus*

## Factfile

| | |
|---|---|
| **Habitat** | Mountain forest, woodland |
| **Distribution** | Mexico, Central and South America |
| **Length** | 11.8 to 13 in |
| **Weight** | 5.3 to 5.6 oz |
| **Life span** | Up to 11 years |
| **Migration** | Nonmigrant |

**Diet** The emerald toucanet has a varied diet. It enjoys feeding on a wide variety of fruit as well as several species of invertebrates and small vertebrates.

**Fact** The emerald toucanet is the most widely distributed of all toucan species. It can be found in many mountainous regions, from Mexico to Venezuela.

**Conservation status**     **Least concern**

# Keel-billed Toucan
## *Ramphastos sulfuratus*

## Factfile

| | |
|---|---|
| **Habitat** | Forest |
| **Distribution** | Mexico, Central and South America |
| **Length** | 17 to 22 in |
| **Weight** | 13 to 18 oz |
| **Life span** | Up to 20 years |
| **Migration** | Nonmigrant |

**Diet** The diet of keel-billed toucans consists mostly of a wide range of fruit, but may also include insects, eggs, nestlings and some small reptiles.

**Fact** When eating fruit the keel-billed toucan uses its large bill to cut up the fruit and then tosses its head back to swallow the pieces whole.

| **Conservation status** | **Near threatened** |
|---|---|

121

# Speckled Mousebird
*Colius striatus*

## Factfile

| | |
|---|---|
| **Habitat** | Forest, woodland, urban areas |
| **Distribution** | Africa |
| **Length** | 12 to 15.5 in |
| **Weight** | 1.6 to 2.7 oz |
| **Life span** | Up to 15 years |
| **Migration** | Nonmigrant |

**Diet** This is a mostly frugivorous bird, meaning the majority of its diet is made up of fruit, however it also eats some leaves, buds and nectar.

**Fact** Mousebirds have reversible outer toes, which gives them the versatility to hang upside down, to climb tree trunks and to walk on the ground.

**Conservation status**     **Least concern**

# Common Wood Pigeon
### *Columba palumbus*

## Factfile

| | |
|---|---|
| **Habitat** | Woodland, farmland, urban areas |
| **Distribution** | Europe, Africa, Asia |
| **Length** | 15 to 17.5 in |
| **Weight** | 10.5 to 22 oz |
| **Life span** | Up to 3 years |
| **Migration** | Partial migrant |

**Diet** Wood pigeons are mainly herbivores, feeding on flowers, leaves, seeds, herbs, grasses, grain and berries, but they also occasionally eat invertebrates.

**Fact** Though wood pigeon is the most common name, this bird is also sometimes known as the woody, cushat, cushy-do, quist, ringdow and ring dove.

| **Conservation status** | **Least concern** |
|---|---|

# Rock Dove

*Columba livia*

Birds

Perching birds and relatives

Pigeons and doves

## Factfile

| | |
|---|---|
| **Habitat** | Cliffs, coast, urban areas |
| **Distribution** | The Americas, Africa, Europe, Asia, Australia |
| **Length** | 11.8 to 14.2 in |
| **Weight** | 9 to 13 oz |
| **Life span** | 3 to 5 years |
| **Migration** | Nonmigrant |

**Diet**
Rock doves, or pigeons, eat seeds, fruit, and some invertebrates. In urban areas they eat food left by people, such as breadcrumbs.

**Fact**
Rock doves can find their way home, even if released from a distant location blindfolded. They navigate by sensing the earth's magnetic fields.

| **Conservation status** | **Least concern** |
|---|---|

# Eurasian Collared Dove

### *Streptopelia decaocto*

## Factfile

| | |
|---|---|
| **Habitat** | Woodland, farmland, urban areas |
| **Distribution** | Europe, Asia, northeast Africa |
| **Length** | 12 to 13.4 in |
| **Weight** | 5.3 to 7 oz |
| **Life span** | Up to 3 years |
| **Migration** | Partial migrant |

**Diet** Collared doves mainly eat seeds and grains such as millet, milo, sunflower, wheat and corn. They also eat some berries, plants and invertebrates.

**Fact** They drink by submerging their bills and sucking water, while most other birds scoop water and tip the head back to let it run into the throat.

| **Conservation status** | **Least concern** |
|---|---|

# Glossary

**Apex predator** An animal with no natural predators within its ecosystem. Apex predators are at the top of their food chains.

**Barbed** Hooks or sharp bristles.

**Bill** A set of narrow protruding jaws without teeth.

**Camouflage** Coloring or patterns that allow an animal to blend in with their surroundings.

**Carrion** The remains of dead animals.

**Cephalopod** A mollusk with a distinct head with large eyes and a ring of tentacles around a beaked mouth. Examples include octopuses, squid and cuttlefish.

**Clutch** A nest of eggs.

**Crustaceans** Arthropods such as lobsters or crabs with jointed legs and two pairs of antennae.

**Diurnal** Active during the daytime.

**Ecosystem** A specific group of organisms (animals and plants) and their environment.

**Frugivorous** An animal that feeds on fruit.

**Grazing** Feeding on grass.

**Ground feeder** An animal that finds food at ground level.

**Habitat** The natural home of a species.

**Herbivore** An animal that feeds on plants.

**Incubating** Maintaining a constant temperature during the development of an embryo.

**Insectivore** A carnivore that eats insects.

**Intertidal zone** The area of foreshore and seashore that is above water at low tide and underwater at high tide.

**Invertebrates** A group of animals without backbones.

**Krill** Small crustaceans that are found in all the world's oceans.

**Limb** A body part, such as an arm, leg or wing.

**Mammals** Warm-blooded vertebrates that suckle their young with milk and have a single bone in their bottom jaw.

**Migrant** An animal that journeys to a different region, following a well-defined route.

**Mollusk** A soft-bodied invertebrate such as a snail, often with a hard protective shell.

**Monochromatic** Male and female members of a species that look identical.

**Monomorphic** Male and female members of a species that behave identically.

**Nocturnal** Active at night.

**Nomadic** Having no fixed home and moving according to the seasons from place to place searching for food, water and grazing land.

**Omnivore** An animal that feeds on plant and animal matter.

**Partial migrant** Animal species in which some populations migrate while others don't.

**Plains** An area of land that is flat or gently rolling.

**Plumage** The patterns, color and arrangement of feathers covering a bird.

**Prairie** An extensive plain of land covered mainly by grass, which in its natural state has deep, fertile soil.

**Prey** An animal hunted and eaten by predators.

**Reptile** One of about 6,000 animal species that breathe air, are cold-blooded and have scaly bodies.

**Riparian** Relating to the banks of a natural course of water.

**Savannah** Hot grasslands in Africa.

**Scavenger** An animal that feeds on refuse and other decaying organic matter.

**Species** A group of animals that are capable of breeding and producing offspring that look like themselves.

**Steppe** A dry, grassy plain that occurs in temperate climates.

**Taiga** Forest that exists as a nearly continuous belt of coniferous trees across North America and Eurasia.

**Tundra** Treeless regions found in the Arctic and on the tops of mountains, where the climate is cold and windy, and rainfall is rare.

**Vertebrate** An animals with a backbone or spinal column. Examples include fish, amphibians, reptiles, birds and mammals.

# Index

Acorn Woodpecker **116**
Adélie Penguin **14**
African Darter **48**
African Grey Parrot **101**
African Spoonbill **61**
Atlantic Puffin **66**
Bald Eagle **76**
Barn Owl **82**
Black Swan **41**
Black-eared Grebe **71**
Blue Jay **92**
Blue-footed Booby **46**
Brown Pelican **45**
Burchell's
  Sandgrouse **24**
California Quail **22**
Canada Goose **34**
Cape Barren Goose **32**
Chinstrap Penguin **15**
Common Buzzard **79**
Common Crane **65**
Common Cuckoo **106**
Common Kingfisher **117**
Common Loon **44**
Common Merganser **40**
Common Moorhen **50**
Common Ostrich **8**
Common Pheasant **21**
Common Swift **111**
Common Wood
  Pigeon **123**
Eastern Kingbird **88**
Egyptian Goose **35**
Emerald Toucanet **120**
Emperor Penguin **13**
Emu **11**
Eurasian Collared
  Dove **125**
Eurasian
  Oystercatcher **51**
Eurasian Teal **39**
Eurasian Wren **95**

European Herring
  Gull **52**
European Nightjar **86**
European Robin **96**
Galah **105**
Golden Eagle **75**
Gray Partridge **19**
Great Cormorant **47**
Great Crested Grebe **70**
Great Egret **62**
Great Hornbill **112**
Great Horned Owl **84**
Great Spotted
  Woodpecker **115**
Great Tinamou **20**
Great Tit **94**
Greater Flamingo **54**
Greater Rhea **9**
Greater Roadrunner **107**
Greater Sage-grouse **23**
Green Heron **56**
Grey Crowned Crane **64**
Grey Heron **57**
Greylag Goose **33**
Harpy Eagle **74**
Helmeted
  Guineafowl **25**
House Sparrow **97**
Humboldt Penguin **18**
Indian Peafowl **30**
Japanese Waxwing **90**
Java Sparrow **98**
Keel-Billed Toucan **121**
Laughing
  Kookaburra **119**
Lesser Flamingo **55**
Little Auk **53**
Little Penguin **17**
Macaroni Penguin **16**
Magpie Goose **31**
Mallard **38**
Mandarin Duck **37**
Muscovy Duck **36**
Mute Swan **42**
New Zealand Fantail **91**

North Island Brown
  Kiwi **12**
Northern Cardinal **99**
Northern Goshawk **77**
Northern Raven **93**
Osprey **73**
Painted Bunting **100**
Peregrine Falcon **80**
Pied Kingfisher **118**
Plain Chachalaca **29**
Purple Swamphen **49**
Rainbow Lorikeet **103**
Red Junglefowl **28**
Red Kite **78**
Red-and-green
  Macaw **102**
Red-crested Turaco **108**
Red-throated Loon **43**
Resplendent
  Quetzal **114**
Rock Dove **124**
Ruby-throated
  Hummingbird **109**
Scarlet Ibis **60**
Shoebill **63**
Snow Petrel **69**
Snowy Owl **83**
Southern Cassowary **10**
Southern Giant Petrel **68**
Speckled Mousebird **122**
Sulphur-crested
  Cockatoo **104**
Superb Fairy-wren **89**
Sword-billed
  Hummingbird **110**
Tawny Frogmouth **87**
Tawny Owl **85**
Turkey Vulture **81**
Violaceous Trogon **113**
Wandering Albatross **67**
Western Barn Owl **82**
Western Capercaillie **27**
Western Grebe **72**
White Stork **59**
Wild Turkey **26**
Wood Stork **58**